her saturn return

her saturn return

mallory huffstetler

WALNUT STREET
—PUBLISHING—

ISBN: 979-8-9909790-7-9

Walnut Street Publishing
1673 S Holtzclaw Ave
Chattanooga, TN 37404

Dedication

This book is dedicated to my one true angel in life, Sanda Bricker. I love you forever and always, my granny girl.

To my dad in spirit, who guided me through each page as my yellow butterfly.

To my husband Charles, who supports all of my wild endeavors, thank you for your never-ending love and support.

be delusional
stay curious
love hard
have the audacity
have the courage to be misunderstood

To the ones who truly see me,
Thank you.

introduction

This is your chance to witness me believing in myself. My
hope is that it will encourage you to do the same. My
inspiration behind this collection of poetry lies in
nature, love, grief, friendship, family, a bit of neuro
spiciness, and a sprinkle of feminine rage. These words are
how I've processed a lot of emotion along with current and
past trauma. This is a witness and testament to my never-
ending healing journey.

Two years ago, I discovered that I really enjoyed writing
poetry. It's the former emo girl turned poet pipeline; what
can I say? In a world where emotions are so discouraged,
I've found healing in writing. It has saved me time and
time again, especially as I navigate through my first
Saturn Return.

Speaking of, a Saturn Return occurs once every 27-30 years
when the planet Saturn returns to the same position in the
sky it was in when a person was born. This lasts for around
three years.

Why is this significant? During this time period, I'd say…
life completely flips upside down. You begin to question
everything that you've known until this point, whether that
be relationships, friendships, or even beliefs you've held
on to your whole life.

While it doesn't always feel wonderful, it is essential and
can be viewed as a rebirth of sorts. This is the perfect
time to reevaluate and discover what is and isn't working
for you and what you'd like to carry into the next chapter
of life.

trigger warning

There are some hard-to-read topics ahead. I have included
trigger warnings (TW) at the top of any poem necessary.
Sometimes I drop the F-bomb. There will not always be
perfect use of grammar. Some things may be spelled
incorrectly. I am very much a believer that poetry is art,
and there's no wrong way to do it.

On the lighter side, I have included what I like to call
"dance breaks" for little tidbits and advice.

awakening.

Like this set of poetry, life is a series
of awakenings. As I frequently like to say,
"Do your best until you know better."
Question everything. Stay curious.

retrograding

she blames her attitude
on how the planets happen to be
a l i g n e d
  (retrograding)
fragile as
pearlescent
    butterflies
with their
    glass wings
dreaming in
  flowering trees
coffee stains on
    book pages
  sweeping
watercolor brushes into
glittering vases
    found light
filtering through
  i'll take photographs
 until you see
yourself
  the way i do

healing isn't linear

the crack in the generations caused
immense
 joy   pain   hurt   growth
self
    discovery
with only great hurt
can one experience
these forms of generational
   h e a l i n g
shattering the glass
of those traumas that
settled in
without asking
without permission
attached by simply being born
like an eye color
or   freckles
 it's part of me
              of you

while healing sounds peaceful
it is anything but
it's funny how much growth
hurts in the process
but leaves you with
 the necessary
              steps to move
                         forward
 bittersweet
a shift in perspective
 healing isn't linear
be gentle
you can change your mind
get triggered
temporarily forget
that doesn't mean
all is lost
every part is progress
every part is important
for all the lives you've
 touched
for all the lives you've changed

me existing is not your permission

it's the way we've been told
  to hide everything
  like bra straps
        & panty lines
but if we don't wear them
        we're sluts
          as if
what we're born with is somehow
      shameful
        lustful
when the only thing despicable
  about this whole ordeal
are the people that make us disguise ourselves
  so they're not
        tempted
as the lack of a bra
  or existing
      apparently
equals an invitation

jack and coke

for thirteen years i made myself
digestible
in the form of the too fun
party girl painfully awkward
finally seen
still stuck in
the version i saw myself in fifth grade
a girl who spoke with
passion about the things she loved
not yet afraid of being judged
they snickered behind my back
forever stunting me
within the version they saw
so i took to liquid courage
dancing on tables
saying those things that should
only be t h o u g h t
then experienced a new form
of bullying
the silent kind
where my friends
were still laughing at me
the kind where i woke up and hated myself
a little more each time

better in community

everything they speak
    that's wrong
with me
is
what makes me
how could
e v e r y t h i n g
about me
    be wrong
    &
why is it
that when i embrace
            encourage
  these parts of myself
        they say
                "me too"
as if
    being me
helps them
to see themselves

choose to see yourself
    so others have the
        courage to do so too

personality

i'm tired of
aesthetic
nothing original ever came from
 white walls
white washed
i want
evergreen
the colors of the
forrest
 i want
ocean blues
the colors of
turquoise seas
give me
purple
the color of
violets
so deep and
royal
 rich
browns
the color of delightfully
creamy coffee
 bright
reds of the native
birds that reside
cardinal moons
fluorescent bright
conformity isn't for me

for lo.

for her i have to make it

  the safe space

that i needed

not everything

  is meant for you

to carry

question beliefs

pay attention to the way it feels

  in your body

listen to yourself

  honor yourself

that is the way

let go or be dragged

alone
yet around others 24/7
connecting to many
seeing bits and pieces in each
screaming
* silently to understand more deeply*
why they choose to come back
holding on to past lives
fought tooth and nail to unfold
no longer those versions
although forever within
flashbacks and nightmares
of suits once worn
kindly
evolve to love the person before you
or
*   l e t   m e   g o*

my life is a masquerade

old soul
  or
forced to learn
 the harshness of
  the world
 before
speaking age
what choice did
 they actually have
  but to live in
 survival from then
     on
  this society
wasn't formed for
 people like them
so they layered
 mask
     upon
        mask
until the person
 standing before you
was socially acceptable
  sure
 the mask still slips
 at times
exposing their true state
   (of constant panic)
 merely to form
      the newest cloak
 blending into their
surroundings
          yet
            again

10

originality

shine

they'll use it

against you

and say

it's your

weakness

just to

dull you

take it

and call it

their own

build a muse

you put me on a pedestal
just to carelessly
tip it
when something
more shiny is revealed
you built me up
this whole idea of who i am
and
who i should be

when the party's over
i've molded myself
into the girl
you always dreamed

you'll see
soon enough
i'm a fraud searching for love
in all directions with the lights off

i slip through like i always will
i require too much
i'm too sensitive
heaven forbid me of having needs
that don't show
up as a whisper
but loud and insistent

i'm not your muse

she will prevail

walking through the mall
with all of its familiar sights
and scents
some things never change
if i could go back to the girl
that relished in a mall run
and tell her where we are today
i would start with the good things
tell her how incredible she's become at
following her dreams
she became an artist
she bought a house
she married her best friend
not perfect but finally
aligned
& then i would have to break the news about dad
about how scary the world can be
how drugs
implanted by the powerful
and grief
wreak havoc on her loved ones
how friends turn to strangers
for no reason of her own
but maybe
we could leave that out
and leave her with optimism
hope
tell her how no matter what
happens
she will p r e v a i l

dance break

to-do list in times of sadness

1. feel
2. cry for as long as needed
3. reach out to a soul friend
4. therapy. whatever that means to you
5. grab all of your favorite snacks
6. have an iced latte if that's your jam. more espresso less depresso. *(but really you should probably have a water and a calming tea instead *grumble grumble*)*
7. pls do not under any circumstances watch the following movies:
Me Before You
About Time
A Star is Born (with lady gaga, duh)
(or do and circle back to #2)
8. make a silly feel-good playlist
9. dance
10. snuggle with your emotional support animal
11. pls do watch: rom coms *(specifically 90s early 2000s)*
12. read a happy book. (I recommend House in the Cerulean Sea by T.J. Klune iykyk)
13. ground in nature
14. cook a super yummy meal
15. give yourself grace and don't judge your feelings

time is a gift

if i could visit my younger self
i would go back to a day when
sharing a laugh with my dad was a given something i never
realized i would have to go a day without

i would go back to the day i gained the strength and
bravery of a lion
i wonder if there was a defining moment or rather a
lifetime of moments and forks in the road

i would go back to the first time i discovered blue
oh how the many impacts that color will have over my life
from the many pools of water i've had the privilege of
experiencing over the summers of my life
the lakes
rivers
and oceans

i would go back to the day that i saw my first glimmer of
hope in symbolism
a yellow butterfly floating across my vision
i would bottle that hope if i could

i would go back to the day where i laid in the grass on an
old family quilt with my best friend
at our favorite park after eating sushi and drinking lattes
simply staring at the clouds dreaming about our future and
what it would be like

i would go back to those critical moments that left a
permanent impact
like him showing me with his actions that i am not good
enough
that there was better out there
i would tell myself that the strength and beauty that is
the gem inside of me can't so easily be chiseled by someone
who won't even lead a critical part in my life
despite the lasting hurt

reversing the clock is not an option offered though
be present

controlled narratives

adolescent life
 forbidden a mystery
young but sure within the walls of
fourth period
 a glimpse
and the text tones of safety
undiscovered
ninth grade
before things got serious
 and the world got so real
a friendship i couldn't
accept
the pillar of
 romance
i sometimes still reflect
will this current
version get to experience
 passion
like it was before
i h a r d e n e d
    exactly
like how i pictured
 pure magic
  young love
that hasn't been damaged yet
by prejudice
and old world reflections
 pure love
only for you and i
ending exactly how i
feared
damaged by those
who claimed to have taught
me all about l o v e
 how could i be wrong
for loving
            someone

sitting here today

i feel sad and
  yes
i'll always wonder
about the gardens
our hearts could have
  grown
without the false
pretenses of
  right and wrong
made up rules
  cut short
  my earliest
        novel

solar power for the rich

until we are all
e q u a l
 we'll never see the rat race
they've put us in
 don't you understand
it isn't about us at all
  we feed
   them our own
  personal energy
solar power
    for the rich
just to
s u r v iv e
they raise the cost
just to blame it on us
for our consumption
of avocado toast
and iced espresso
because they say
you poor things
you don't even deserve
 the small luxuries
we want to
take that too

mother

neon green of willow leaves
steady promises of flowing water
        vibrant yellows
wild   violets
        native plants
if
  we allow
      growth

like we're
      entitled
they grew here first
we came   next

destruction

if we let her
she can h e a l us

instead

we choose following
the ones that kill us
for more p o w e r
it will
   never
      be
         enough

if only we would
r e m e m b e r
our roots
just like the willow
   the wild violets
we have everything
that we need
   within us

we are the same

before power told us we needed
t h i n g s

to complete us

we are not gaining
but giving them

more

    more

       more

we will only thrive
in togetherness
in community

if only we could see

feeling.

Being able to name your feelings can help
you to communicate more thoroughly and
effectively. Most only think of 3 to 4
different emotions (ex. happy, sad, mad.)
But we are so much more complex than that,
my friend.

anxiety attack

it manifests first in my chest
felt
in my lungs
my mouth
as i breathe deeply
 anxiety
in my throat
feels
like a blockage it
prevents me from
speaking freely
 i will hold my breath to
take up less
(space)
it feels like an unfinished sentence

i imagine moving
out
the negative
and breathing in only
l i g h t
one day at a time
one moment at a time

hurt personified

to the parts of me that are still hurting
i acknowledge you
i feel you
you are an ever prevalent part of who i am you are part of
my experience
you have been here my entire life
one of my very few constants
although most would view you as a negative
i actually contribute much of my strength to you
in all areas of my life
currently i am referring to the parts of me who are still
experiencing you
hurt
the funny thing is how we wish to bury you
when all you need is to to be heard
to be felt
and suddenly i wake up
refreshed reborn healed
i am still experiencing past traumas
the hurt that shouldn't sting as much as it currently does
i am still hurting from the grief of losing those who i
assumed would live forever
i am still discovering new things that bring you to me
like a friendship not quite being
what i expected
like assuming another has the same heart as you
like assuming the world and people are as good as you give
them the chance to be
i am hurting from the things that have not quite happened
yet
anxiety
to the parts of me who are still hurting
i acknowledge you
i accept you
i hear you
soon we will sit together
process grow heal

pain

we tend to avoid it
  (pain)
mostly
when i feel it
for just a moment
 i feel relief
for a fleeting time
i have a feeling that can be comprehended
 empathized with
unlike in those times of deep grief
and depression
when they just say "i'm so sorry"
with blank looks of panic
we don't know how to support our friends in need
when it gets uncomfortable
i get it
what do you say
in the face of grief
 that could possibly change the
outcome
you don't
you just see with your heart
and say
"i am here"

engulfed

passion
looks like
a bright flame
at first sight
it may b u r n your eyes
   wants to engulf
 and enamor you
sounds like an
upbeat tempo leading
   to a climax
reminds me why i
am allowed to take up
space
when it touches me
 it pulls me >in<
mirroring me
 a flame so fervent
helplessly capturing
 everything it touches
i let it consume
imagine how far it

will go

JealouSea

hindered
     by a green eye
 "why do you do that"
thoughts of
      insecurity
don't you see
  a shine dulled
  doesn't mean
yours will be more
   fluorescent
  waves of emerald
you
   killed
      her
        dream

confidence

leo   scorpio
    gemini
oh my
don't worry she's
divine
yet
an unreliable narrator
if you ask her why
she'll say
it's the gemini moon
that gives her two
faces
and when she goes distant
you'll hear
her drop scorpio rising
she walks
in the room with an
air of confidence
oxygen fanning the flame
(she's faking it)
but if you call out her dauntless
a u r a she'd say
it's natural
i'm a leo

unhealed men

the first time

i chased someone

incapable

of love

he taught me how to be

u s e d

i got to

re-write my story

only after being a prompt

for

u n h e a l e d

men

Dance Break

Did you know that everyone is creative? Yes, YOU. This doesn't have to mean painting, poetry, crafting, the usual suspects when we think "creative." If you ask me, even though I experience dyscalculia and numbers make my brain all fuzzy, I think math is SO creative. That's just one example. I highly encourage you to create in whatever manner, however that may look for you.

Going back to the usual suspects... I am genuinely such a *literal* person due to my neuro-spiciness.
I always thought I needed to be taught the proper, most perfect way of doing things. I never liked the art that I created because I didn't think it was "good enough." But to whose standards?

As I got older, I realized that the fun in art is that... there are no rules! If you love what you produce, and it's created authentically from the heart, THAT is truly all that matters. Now, you'll find my art in every crevice of my home, and I absolutely adore it.

Will everyone love it? Probably not. Our art is not for everyone though. It's for those who need to see it and sometimes just for ourselves.

Have the audacity to create and the vulnerability to share. You never know who may need to see it. The only thing you need to know before you get started is that to create all you have to do is just start. Start somewhere. Start anywhere! You and your art in any form whether it be on a canvas, paper, word form, number form, etc. are so beautiful and worthy.

when ts said "i'm a nightmare dressed
like a daydream"

"you will find better
than me"
that's all
after the vulnerability
 stripped to my
shadow

now i'm too much
didn't need
a crystal ball
 to see

"you're my dream"
they always say
"everything but more"
 then they learn
exactly what
e v e r y t h i n g
   encompasses

messy | raw | emotional | needy
  you see through the cracks

 7 years
  of bad luck
you know
    is
    leaving a woman
     scorned
            xoxo

TW: Sexual Assault

betrayed

unconscious
the state of me when you decided
it was your right to touch me
 entitlement of my
b o d y you even told me
the next day like it was some
s e c r e t
i never agreed to be
part of as if the words
that i spoke could give you
permission
for something you knew
wasn't okay
even photographed it
so you'd have memory of
deceit and
            <u>assault</u>
but that wasn't what it was
                        to y o u
i was so
young and
you took advantage
 made me think just
because we were together that you
were
     a l l o w e d
 but
just so you know
  i'm older now
i no longer keep your sick
     s e c r e t
because i know another
needs to hear how not okay
that was

TW: Suicidal Ideation

tsunami

the birds are
 chirping
        outside
while i'm
dying
            inside
begging
 to be loved
& understood
     how
when
i mask every day
no one knows who i am
because i should
 be a good girl

        not rock the boat

i want to flip it
   tsunami

      drown
the limitations that
have been forced upon me
   wield lightning
     release the torture
   & pain this life
has inflicted
i didn't ask for this
 don't even want to be
          here

i exist to
         please

     i wish this world
could keep the loving touch
     i've left

while erasing myself from my
loved one's minds
so they can keep going
& i can cease

instead i'll
put on my setting spray
continue the day
  goddess forbid
the tear streaks distract
from the conventional beauty
i was gifted
by two parents who
no longer speak

grieving.

We often view grief as black and white.
grieving the loss of a loved one. But what
about the future you planned for? What
about the career you thought you'd have? A
relationship you dreamed of? What about the
friendship you lost? We experience grief
over many things in life. Being able to
recognize it can help you to fully
experience it, reduce shame surrounding it,
help you to heal, and recognize what you're
going through.

Unrequited

i reach for you
 you reach for me
        simultaneously
  stepping backwards
just out of my g r a s p
just like my touch on reality
unrequited love
though
you're too much
of a coward to say
you hope i'll stay
  anyway
hanging onto coattails
nose under the bubbles
of a french 75
you aren't yet in the space
  to receive
the timing is wrong
 you'll say
a mirror of everything
within me
  don't worry
you have me for a while longer
there's nothing i love more
   than loving
the souls who aren't
 capable of
    loving me too

maybe

maybe
in an alternate universe
that thing never happened to us
 as little girls &
we grew up healthy and happy
 maybe
we got to be innocent for just a
 while longer &
wonder and imagination were our
normal not just a method
of escape to forget our surroundings
 maybe
we were nurtured and encouraged to
form strong bonds with our friends
over more than just shared
 trauma &
we bonded over our matching
eyes and favorite artists
 maybe
in an alternate universe
 i could be safe &
 i could be enough

hanami

i fear so
  that when you depart
      i will follow
inevitably there's a piece of
  me that only exists while you
  walk the earth
sitting under the cherry blossom
      near the spring
contemplating
              dreaming
in budding blooms
  each flower fallen rapidly
such as our   mortality
how the time we assume we have
      can dissipate as quickly as
  the tree that takes a year to bloom
  for such a short period
  how we don't appreciate each
  sacred petal enough before fallen
while here I'll pour endearment
  into your floral leaves
              saturate
  all of the details and colors of your
          nature
although existence is
      ephemeral
how you've touched the lives of many
      permanently
  to be remembered with pure
  intention
          and gratitude
for my existence is proof of the
kindness your everlasting
    touch will provide

i'm in the spring of my life

a newly emerged flower

  petals of pastel hues

    soft as the healing

      has begun to allow me to be

as the floral spring i'll only

  be here for a while too

my petals will fall

  touching the floors of

my loved ones

  i hope they'll remember

  beauty once shared

& that while my spring may

have ended

there will always be another

just as beautiful

vibrant

  achingly alive

as i once was

angels | mcb

standing at the edge of the water
next to your brother

a lump in our chest
neither acknowledging
but feeling
the giant piece of us we lost
in July
wings guide us

yellow butterfly

floating past
a sign from you
we're not alone

you told us
we never would be

yellow butterfly

i know that love is real
for the reason that you came back
in the form of my favorite
yellow butterfly after i planted
gold roses begging for you to exist
once again
you float along
the creek in front of my house
where you came to her in a dream
& when i'm unsure
i see you flutter past
my window
letting me know that
it's okay
to go forward
that you're proud of me
& support everything that i do

i love you

maury matters

no one warns you
as a child
the justice system only works
if you're the right
color
or
an upstanding citizen

& now i understand
just how privileged i have been

they don't care
when you've been misled
by big pharma
when you become an addict
after a back surgery

the pills
numbed the pain
until you didn't
e x i s t anymore
& no one stopped to find out why

he did it to himself
they'll say
just to die alone
because the people
he called his friends
were too scared about
their own misconduct
to be sure his
story came to light

grieving the loss of the living

we focus so solely in on the loss
of romantic partners
what about
best friends
the ones who you were your
most raw
most vulnerable
now you're just strangers
a polite compliment here and there
if that
but
I
bared my truths
to you
my veils
completely dropped
lost
slowly
i felt it
my guards
back up
this may be the last time
you
the last person
i ever let in that deeply
again
misplaced trust
miscommunication
misunderstood
the grief
of the friendship we
dreamed about

unsustainable

so much you taught me
so much that i am thankful for
if you called me today i wouldn't
pick up
c o e x i s t i n g are
the happiness you gave me
the happiness you r i p p e d away
you decided
i was only worth what i could
give
i loved who i knew you
could be
instead of who you told me
you were
friendship
a fire
that wasn't sustainable

mother wound

i forgive you
now that i'm older
i would like to understand
still hurting from
things i barely remember
a source of your hurt too
purpose
burden
helped me grow more whole
yet still broken
i just needed to hear
"i'm so proud of you"
the love i so desperately
wanted from you
regardless
i made it
i needed you
but
i also forgive you

grief

there are so many
  e x p e c t a t i o n s
how long it should last
 when you should be
      over it
as if grief
ever gave a fuck
about our timelines
  and presuppositions
no one warns you
it almost never happens right after
      the loss occurs
rather when
the sun is shining
 and you realize you
  can't share your
last pint of ice cream
  their favorite indulgence
you have car trouble
and the one person that
has all of the answers
 can no longer speak them
when you dial their number
 just to be met with
 "this number is no
      longer in service"

home.

Sometimes in life we are farther from
ourselves than we realize. My healing
journey has been all about self-discovery
and coming home to myself.

see me

i have this wound
it's constantly shouting
  "see me see me"
when i was a girl
   they looked away
& i made myself small
to fit into
the corners of safety
 i got older
the wound screamed
 louder
calling in more of those
behind their blindfold
i took claim on every inch
of space i could manage
 in the house i built
i lit a candle
   made it home
& decided to
 to see myself

dance break

In my healing era I discovered a few books that really changed the game for me.

Homecoming by Thema Bryant. This is where I discovered the whole concept of coming home to myself.

Unmasking Autism by Decon Price. This book helped me understand the way my brain works and why I've felt out of place my entire life. (Side note: it has a ton of helpful information about not only autism but ADHD and other neurospiciness.)

Atlas of the Heart by Brené Brown. Honestly, anything by Brené is bible but this book, in particular, is so helpful for understanding emotions and learning to name them. So important for any healing journey!

the end

you just had to
e x p e r i e n c e
her
you didn't want to know her
though
once out of line
with the container
| you put her in |
made to look like a castle
you know
the ones with
dragons because
to keep her
you had to fight
with fire
 extinguishing
          identity
we already
know that story

now she's escaped
the weight of what you wanted her to be
shattered

no longer
your
pretty pretty
princess after all

delulu

the magic i've created in alone time
spinning to music
i desperately
wish that you
could hear this too
and join me
it takes time
deprogramming
separation
from all of those
s o c i e t a l expectations
you'll never meet
because it's a never
ending rainbow road
they paved it beautifully
but beneath
all of the primary colors
it's cement t o n e d

my soul is free

i finally
 let go
of everything
 >crushing< my
spirit
gave myself
 [s p a c e]
to just
 b e
the only person
limiting
 m e
false beliefs
 & shame
let g o
 this is my
monarch r e l e a s e

don't give up

i've never felt this way
 bursting with j o y
at the seams
happiness i've chased
finally it
found me
the path is far
 from e a s y
it requires
 loss
pain
 the very death
of who you are if you are brave
enough to hang around
 let me finish
this song
as i take in the lyrics to
strawberry wine by noah kahan
 feeling a burst of passion
for my life i almost gave
up on
after the most l o s s
i have ever experienced
the colors are so
different now

everyone else in the room can see it

screaming at the top of our lungs to songs
that confirm we're young
you looked at me & you said
"this is the way i feel about you"
as harry styles sang
"you don't know you're beautiful"
just like that i giggled
& forgot
only to remember
12 years later and fully understand what you meant
i see it now
my worth
who i am
that i am worthy of being
called beautiful
sweet friend thank you,
i see you too

you're a light

imagine
your name brought up
in a room
where you are
absent

a lovely soul is
encouraging you
speaking in mouthfuls of
sugar and
candied hearts

about all of the magnificence
you put into the world

it's not all doom & gloom
sweet angel

sometimes it comes from
a stranger
rather than a friend

i know how much that hurts
yet
isn't it so beautiful

someone can see that in you
even when you can't

chasing waterfalls

waterfall sprays

  glittering skin

  the rush

sun bursts

  sweet and bright

tangerine dreams

all of it

leading you

          to

              me

finally in harmony

nothing fits quite like the glove
of a love
you had to grow
into
a love so perfectly
curated
you'd think we wrote it ourselves
in a sense
we did
with years of unraveling
our trauma built
in from not only the union
of two but the four
that came before us
i know many who
would have thrown in the towel
that's the tricky part
about not knowing what lies ahead
imagine the premature deaths
of those who couldn't see past
the lack of communication
if you have a little more love
a little more grace
and a lot of patience
left to give someone what they need
to bloom
to see you
to give themselves what
they need
so in return they can nurture you
tenfold then
stop rushing
and give it time

c.w.h.

the same dive bar we always go to
midtown hipsters or so we thought
in town after
moving away
we left it all behind
but never each other
 degenerates together
wild and hot
random but not at all
my soul saw yours
and she whispered after so much despair
let's go
a d v e n t u r e
 how i said in the car
i'd marry you tomorrow and travel everywhere
together
21 and so much to learn
but fuck it
if you're in
so am i what could go wrong
but hurricanes
 pandemics
oceans of pain
but everything to gain
 like the love we share
the mountains we now live between
 a creek flowing so full of the
memories we gush over
 on the porch of our house
 i named arwen

healing mal

who would i be
had i not heard
"at least she's pretty"
as if pretty
were the only valued thing about me
as if my existence were
ever so
shallow who would i be
had i not heard
"she's not the smartest"
said as a minute comment however
a lifetime
it lasted
who would i be had i not heard
"you'll never succeed in that way"
 as if i didn't go on
to do exactly that despite
who would i be had i not heard "have you gained weight?"
or
"have you lost weight?"
followed by
"you look phenomenal"
"skinny queen"
as if the addition or lack thereof
a few extra inches
were the measurement of my goodness flaws morals spirit
knowledge....
 because i can't go back
i will envision her instead
i will embrace her and speak
light kindness
& truth
 "you are safe now"

i am home

my life is
 f l a s h i n g before my eyes
   yet instead of the loving events
shown are the versions of me
   people have met & known

there she is so young trying to fit
precariously
wondering where it will be
she'll be allowed to fill space

 home she belonged out of
   the way and quiet

 she didn't play sports
   art wasn't encouraged
she was convinced she wasn't
   intelligent or interested
 in being an academic scholar
   or maybe would have been
if her teachers hadn't called her t o o slow

regardless that was
 off the table
so where will she go

 she'll start to chase friends
   boys that give her the smallest attention as
she'd been a socially inept outsider yet
all of a sudden that was no longer a reality

she got older and learned
   the added spice of a shot or two
 discovered how to illuminate
the room
 hold them captive

   until she had too much
            unmasked too much

& then they saw her

as messy
   only the good time
girl

who wants to be with her
be her friend
now she's lonely again

today she embraced
   her inner artist with her career

no more shots & becoming a mess
   just to fill spaces

surely they'll finally love
   her now that she's healed
      less rowdy
but
   that drove them away too
they don't know how to handle
   her sober
      too awkward
      not the life of the party they were allured with

         except a few
she calls her soul friends
   community
despite being alike or not
   constant conversational flow
      even quiet moments encouraged
so much space for one another
   warmth
welcomed with open arms
i am home

Her Saturn Return

and in the end
 it's who
stood beside you
 during your

saturn return

i hope you know
 the most important person
will always be

you